Martha's Vineyard
Contemporary Living

KEITH MOSKOW AND ROBERT LINN

Martha's Vineyard | Contemporary Living

THE MONACELLI PRESS

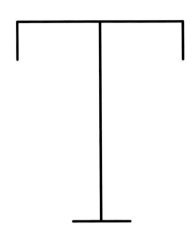

THIS IS OUR SECOND SURVEY of contemporary houses on Martha's Vineyard. The first, The Houses of Martha's Vineyard, featured houses built between 1986 and 2004; here we continue with houses completed over the next five years, the most recent in 2009. This period saw unprecedented growth on the island, held in check by strict zoning by-laws and the Martha's Vineyard Commission's all-encompassing oversight. Without these controls, there is great risk of destroying the island's most alluring features—vistas through open fields to ocean waters, clusters of community buildings, thickets of forest and pastoral agricultural land.

The houses included here expand on the traditional Vineyard vernacular of shingled houses and cottages. Each of the architects has described the goals for the project and the source of the design. Some reference nautical themes, others environmental concerns, and still others appropriateness of materials and scale. A significant number rely on a plan strategy based on a series of pavilions to minimize intrusion in the landscape while still taking advantage of views and prevailing breezes. What links these houses is that they are all built to stand the test of time in the sometimes extreme marine environment, and they respectfully break with tradition.

Those traditions are rooted in the history of Martha's Vineyard, which was first charted by Bartholomew Gosnold for the British Crown in 1602. Gosnold named the island for his daughter and for the wild grapes that blanketed the land. Beginning the mid-seventeenth century, Europeans began to settle the island, supporting their families by fishing and farming. It was not until the mid-nineteenth-century that the Vineyard emerged as a summer resort, spurred by the Methodist Camp Meetings, with islanders and visitors from Boston and New York converging on the area that is now the town of Oak Bluffs.

Despite its popularity as a summer destination, the Vineyard was slow to build hotels or improve roads, and it made no recreational use of its harbors. Summer business withered in the wake of every stock market crash or recession. In the late nineteenth century and the first half of the twentieth century, summer residents came to enjoy a simple life—the only life the Vineyard offered.

By the 1990s, that situation had changed. The year-round population of about 15,000 grew to close to 100,000 in the summer, with an additional 25,000 visitors arriving for the day by ferry. The pressures on the Vineyard to conform to mainland standards of entertainment and comfort have become constant, and preservation groups are vigilant in resisting changes that would compromise the island's character.

The domestic architecture of Martha's Vineyard reflects its colonial history, its prosperity in the nineteenth century, and its emergence as a popular resort. The early English settlers built simple houses—one-story wood-and-shingle structures in keeping with their Puritan beliefs and the challenges of island living. By the early eighteenth century, second stories were added, creating colonial houses. Classically inspired architecture came to the Vineyard during the nineteenth century as whaling captains and investors based primarily in Edgartown sought to demonstrate their success through house building. Unique to Oak Bluffs are the Carpenter Gothic cottages that replaced the tents of the Methodist campgrounds after the Civil War. Rambling shingle style and colonial revival houses, introduced in the early twentieth century, continue to evoke the casual elegance of the Vineyard summer.

While we admire these historic traditional styles—described collectively as the "architecture of the American summer"—we have chosen to study the introduction of a contemporary vocabulary to the island landscape. From the 1960s onward, an intrepid and distinct group of summer residents was attracted to parts of the Vineyard that had historically been less desirable, areas far from the port towns and fertile farmland. These residents were seeking the drama of exposed bluffs and cliffs, the promontories, the outwash plains, and the deep forest, and their architects responded with houses that add a new dimension and perspective to the historic vernacular forms.

Now fifty years old, the "tradition" of contemporary architecture on the Vineyard is established, but the forms and materials continue to evolve in response to changes in life style, technology, and environmental concerns. Extended families, seeking both privacy and community in shared vacation houses, create "great rooms" for living and eating, often opening to generous porches and patios, but designate wings or pavilions as bedrooms and guest quarters with private outdoor space. Sustainable materials, passive ventilation, even prefabrication all contribute to making these houses energy efficient and cost effective to maintain.

The houses presented in this book represent the most current interpretations of contemporary design, aligned with and in some cases tempered by restrictions and controls and responsive to the landscape in which they sit. Today another force, the economic downturn that began with the financial crisis of 2008, has impacted building on the Vineyard, just as it has curtailed construction throughout the world. We cannot predict the long-term effect for the island, but we continue to take pride in the balance between its rich architectural heritage and magnificent natural beauty.

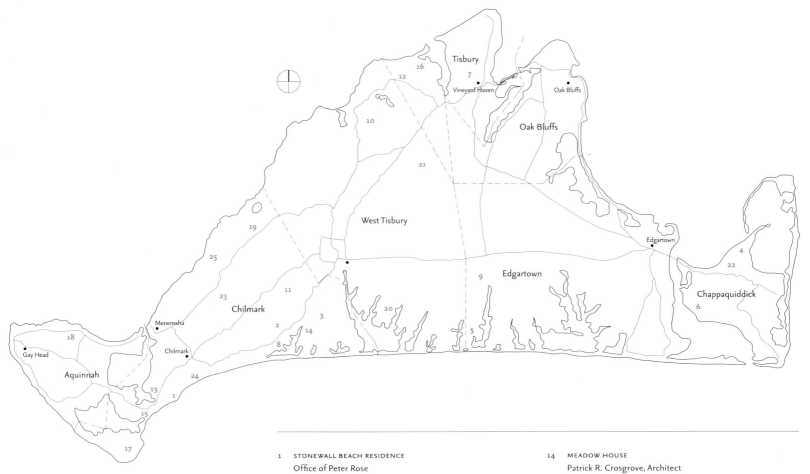

2007

Stonewall Beach Residence | Office of Peter Rose

CHILMARK

S

TONEWALL BEACH RESIDENCE is situated on a small peninsula on the southern coast of the Vineyard. The views from the site are breathtaking. The southerly expanse surveys more than a mile of coastline—waves breaking against a crescent-shaped shore of beaches and cliffs. To the west is tranquil Stonewall Pond.

The house was designed as a retreat for a New York art collector. The plan allows every room a view of the ocean. Windows facing the water are oversized, often going around corners to provide panoramic views of the coast. On bright days, the interior has balanced light and no glare, and even on the gloomiest days, artificial lights are rarely required anywhere in the interior. In the living room, dining room, kitchen, and study, large panels of glass slide open, eliminating all barriers to the sight, sound, and smell of the sea.

Cedar-planked walls are dimensioned with enough width to make space for cabinetry and to conceal doors and sliding partitions. Interior doors swing into this space when open, becoming nearly invisible. Bedroom orientation provides complete visual privacy, so doors are rarely closed, and doorways remain open, cedar-planked passages. Entry and kitchen, and living room and office are separable by moving partitions, which slide or swing into the wall, concealed when open.

With a primary structure mostly of steel, the house is robust, constructed to weather well and be durable. At the same time, it is finely finished and detailed with both the exterior and interiors entirely of wood. Settled into its environment with a stubborn ruggedness, yet fully operable and made to engage the site by slipping out of the way, it is a carefully crafted piece of cabinetry.

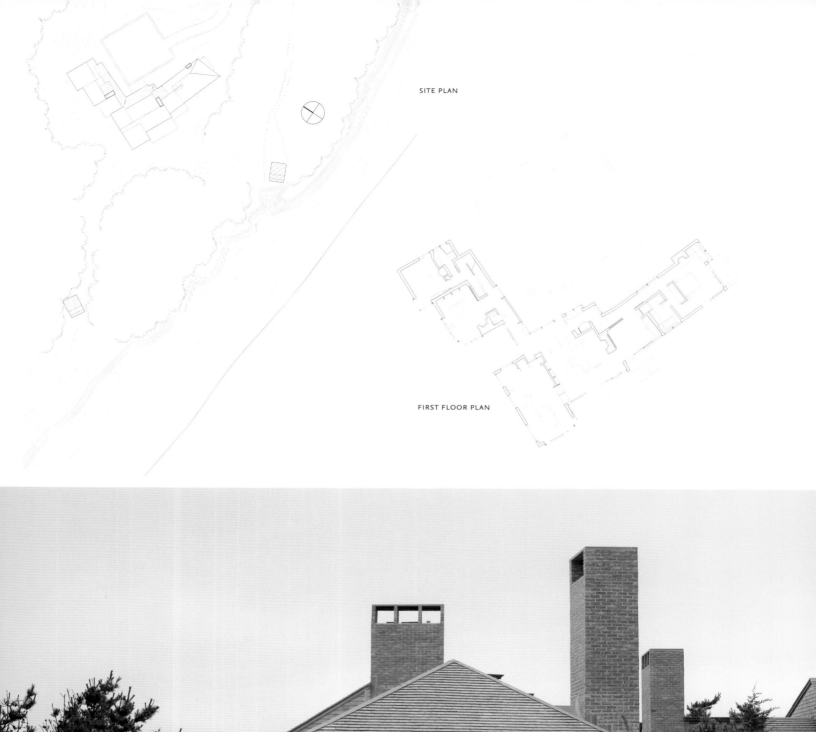

SITE PLAN

FIRST FLOOR PLAN

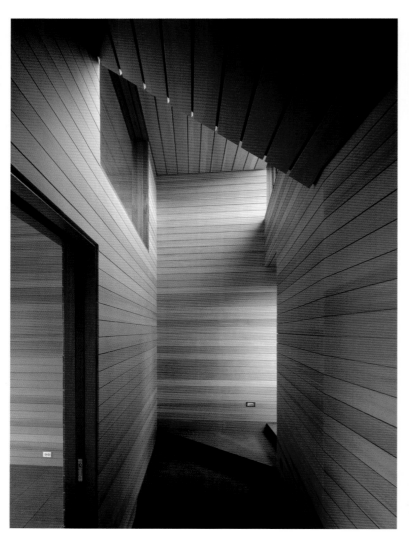

THE DESIGN OF HIGHLAND HOUSE blends traditional Vineyard design motifs with a contemporary aesthetic that feels neither historicist nor out of place. Wood siding and shingles, lead-coated copper and steel sunscreens comprise the simple palette of exterior materials. Some elements—the master bedroom, guestrooms, and garage—are separated from the family gathering areas to provide privacy and create a variety of exterior spaces. These terraces, patios, and screened porches allow the owners to experience the natural setting in all kinds of climatic conditions. Traditional dry-set granite walls are used to organize the site.

An elevated, wood-plank walkway leads to the house. The entry side has nominal openings to preserve privacy and to serve as a counter-point to the openness of the view side of the house. Just outside the front door, the path passes a large erratic (a glacially deposited stone) that is also seen through a slot window in the entry area. A curved ceiling plane spans the length of the central space, which contains the living, dining, and kitchen areas. The interior walls do not reach the ceiling, further accentuating the sense of discovery that the interior volumes are different from the exterior massing.

2006

Highland House | Rick Sundberg/Olson Kundig Architects

CHILMARK

21

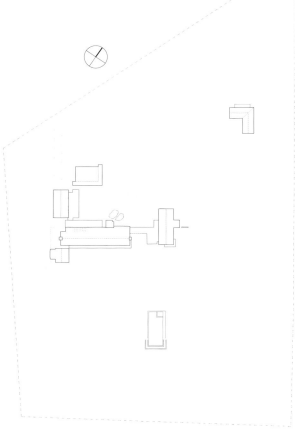

SITE PLAN

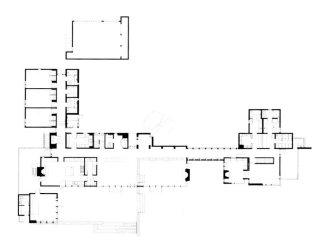

FIRST FLOOR PLAN

MVII | Moskow Linn Architects

CHILMARK

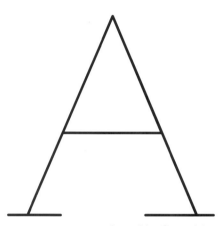

SUMMER RETREAT shared by four siblings and their children, MVII sits on a narrow, six-acre site facing a seagrass meadow. In a setting where there are no views or even a glimpse of the sea, the house is opened to a courtyard and expansive grassy meadowland carved from the scrub oak forest.

An intentionally circuitous journey to the house is a key aspect of the design; the landscape/house composition is revealed slowly. The arrival point is a covered arcade that forms a connecting baseline for the two separate wings of the house. These private and public companion pieces create a roofless enclosure— an outdoor room. More importantly, the long narrow structures frame a view: an allée of trees leading the eye toward the field traversed during the initial approach.

The plan blurs the distinction between inside and out. Covered porches run the length of the wings serving as outdoor hallways. While it is possible to pass from bedroom to bedroom in the sleeping wing, it is much easier to wander along the veranda. The house encourages living out of doors.

Similar to southern "shot gun" houses, the linear design allows for natural ventilation in each room. Ventilation is further enhanced by the orientation of the courtyard to the southwest prevailing breeze. Deep overhangs add to cooling.

Wood, the traditional material for construction on the Vineyard, is used in non-traditional ways with additive porch columns, exposed modular structural members and revealed details. Inside the exposed fir of the floors, ceilings, and trim form a warm neutral backdrop for family life. Green Vermont slate of the massive interior chimney contrasts with the wood. The chimney divides the living room from the kitchen, with gaps between the chimney and wall providing glimpses of each room from the other.

FIRST FLOOR PLAN

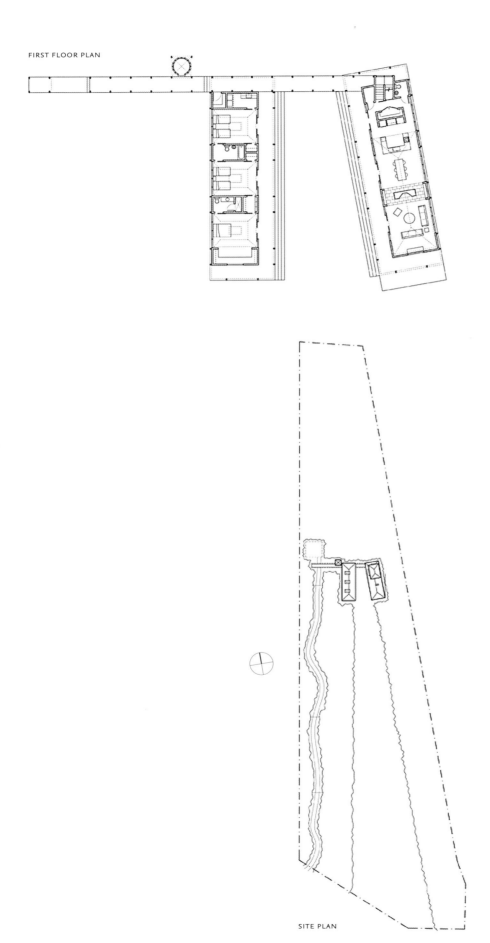

SITE PLAN

2009

Bluff House | Maryann Thompson Architects

CHAPPAQUIDDICK

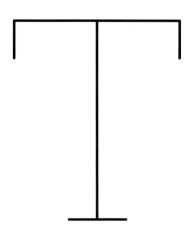

HE IMAGE OF BLUFF HOUSE, with its wide overhangs and wooden interiors, is peaceful and shady, harkening back to the early camps of the Vineyard. Occupying the crest of a windblown bluff overlooking the Atlantic and nearby saltwater ponds, the house situates the occupant between an earthen stone plinth and light trapezoidal roof forms. The complex form is generated by the natural forms of the bluff on which it sits. The house visually becomes an extension of the landscape as the roof planes reciprocate the formal qualities of the bluff, windswept cedars, and cresting waves of the Atlantic below.

The interior layout revolves around the central combined living/dining/kitchen space. Moments of intimacy are achieved within the open floor plan through the use of nooks and smaller spatial moments. The house is laid out organically, in an attempt to heighten the multiple water views and relationships to the site and landscape beyond. The angled floor plan directs views away from neighboring houses and creates a covered exterior sitting area, addressing the ocean and fostering a sense of privacy.

Cedar tongue-and-groove cladding is used for both exterior and interior walls, creating visual continuity and evoking the Vineyard's boat-building traditions.

FIRST FLOOR PLAN

2006

Point House | Hart Associates Architects

EDGARTOWN

POINT HOUSE IS SITED at the end of a peninsula on Oyster Pond in Edgartown. A long dirt drive travels past cottages and pastures to a broad clearing. At the entrance to the site are a large weathered barn, a horse paddock, and an 1800s white clapboard farmhouse. Beyond the original farm buildings, Point House is visible in the distance. The approach to the house passes osprey nests along a cove to the east and a swimming dock to the west. A new barn frames the view of the house and marks the entrance to the gravel entry court.

The house is a cluster of three low-pitched volumes unified by a simple covered porch to the north. The structures are set at angles to follow the topography and views. The main views are to the south. The sun animates each piece as the day progresses. The open plan allows for shared views from one space to the next. All of the living spaces are connected to the views beyond, and the extensive perimeter allows ocean air to filter through the entire house. The play of sparkling light is ever-present as it bounces off the water.

FIRST FLOOR PLAN   SITE PLAN

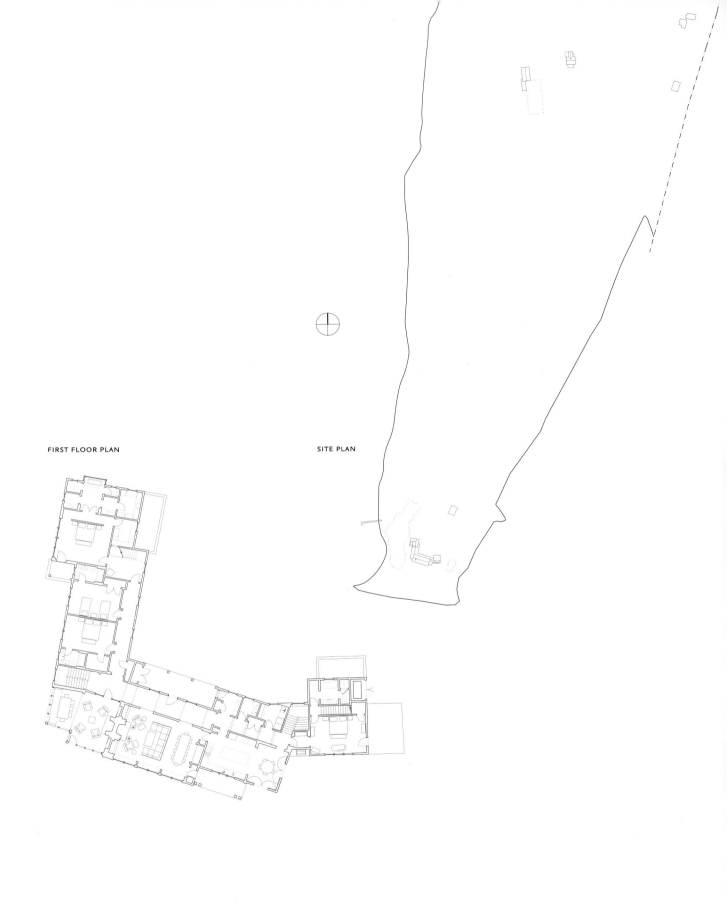

The palette of materials is both traditional and deliberately limited: bleached cedar shingles, over-scaled double-hung windows with crisp casings, wood and metal roofing. The landscape materials are rough-hewn and solid—granite, bluestone, wood decking. The interior carries an echo of the elemental quality of the older buildings on the site—timber framing, concrete, granite, and wide wood flooring. Wall surfaces are rough-sawn wood, hand-rubbed plaster, and crisply colored paint.

Snow Point | Hutker Architects

CHAPPAQUIDDICK

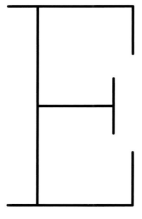

VOKING THE "BOW ROOF" vernacular of Vineyard sailors' cottages, Snow Point sits contentedly on the harbor from a raised stone promontory. A grandfathered proximity to the waterfront mandated that this new house be redeveloped on an existing footprint. The living areas are elevated to take advantage of views and to deal with flood plain issues. From the inland approach, landscaped stone terraces ascend the natural grade to the entry/living level with a panoramic harbor view beyond.

The "life room" has an exposed handcrafted timber frame that expresses the bow roof form. The house is zoned, providing bedroom suites that enjoy quiet autonomy each focused upon differing views. The house can be utilized for full extended-family vacation time, or more intimately, using just the "life room" and master suite during a winter weekend.

Bow roofs by nature provide extra volume at the second floor, critical in achieving second floor areas within the height restrictions. Square dormers update the traditional form.

Natural shingles, stone, metal, and contextual window color, derived from upland bayberry stems and complementing the wetland grasses, are indigenous materials that defer to the surrounding woodlands and passive harbor front.

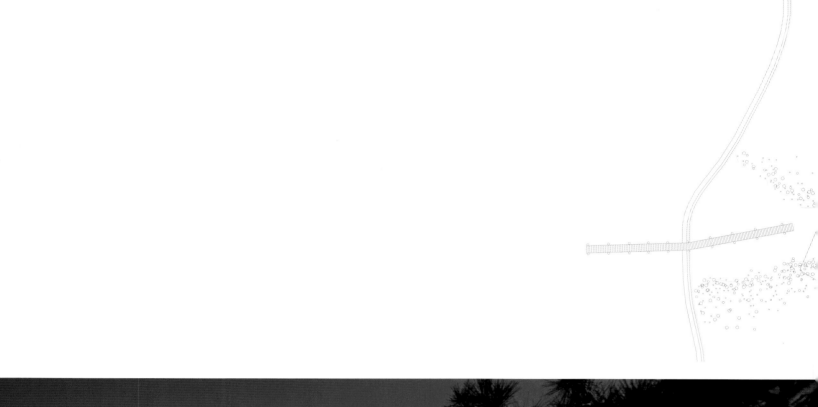

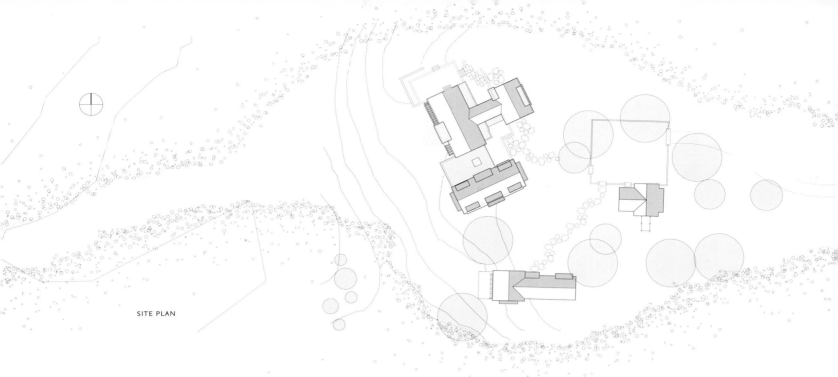

SITE PLAN

FIRST FLOOR PLAN

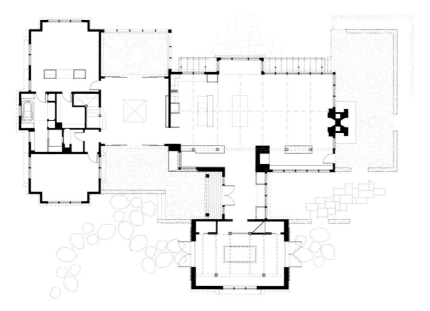

VH R-10 gHOUSE | Darren Petrucci AIA

VINEYARD HAVEN

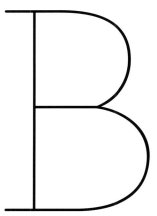

B

UILT TO WITHSTAND the harsh weather of the Vineyard while resting lightly on the land, VH R-10 gHOUSE was designed to overcome the limitations of highly restrictive zoning. The gently sloping property, within walking distance of the town of Vineyard Haven, could accommodate both a main house and a guesthouse. The architect-owners elected to build the guesthouse first, which limited them to a footprint of 600 square feet and a maximum height of 24 feet.

To maximize the allowable envelope, Petrucci drew a 16-by-40-by-24-foot box based on a 4-foot construction module. Structurally insulated panels (SIPs) enclose three staggered, rectilinear volumes for cooking, living, and sleeping. Though the center volume is shifted out four feet to accommodate an exterior stair, a mahogany rain screen unifies the

FIRST FLOOR PLAN

volumes, enveloping the stair and blurring the line between outside and in. The program called for a kitchen, living area, and master bedroom on the main level. The small loft and spacious lower-level guest suite do not count toward the square footage allotted by zoning so, cleverly, 600 technical square feet become 1,000 square feet of livable space. A raised sod-covered roof and deck, accessed by the exterior stair, creates a secluded aerie in the tree canopy.

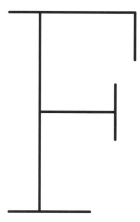

ULLY WRAPPED ON TWO SIDES by Chilmark Pond, and looking out across the barrier beach beyond, this property was home to a tiny, historic camp perched on a bluff. The current owner decided to move the camp about forty feet inland and convert it into the core of her own house, adding two wings perpendicular to one another, each running along one aspect of the pond.

The massing is quiet in a traditional Vineyard style with a cascade of low, shingled roofs. The L-shaped plan follows the profile of the pond and the cove; each room looks out to one or the other. To balance the exposed nature of the property on the water side, an intimate courtyard garden was created in the sheltered area formed by the house and the garage. The interior is open, airy, bright, and spare. The furnishings are quietly contemporary and designed to be subordinate to the views.

Along with the re-use of the existing camp, salvage materials were used extensively throughout the building. The exposed interior collar ties and posts, the fireplace mantel, and the entry porch timber arch are made from native oak trees cleared from various Vineyard sites. The interior and exterior trim, decking, screen doors, and some of the built-ins are made from "sinker" cypress that comes from timber that sunk to river bottoms in the South in the nineteenth century when the old-growth cypress forests were logged. The doors are crafted from redwood that came from dismantled beer tanks at the Narragansett Brewery in Rhode Island.

2001

Pond House | South Mountain Company

CHILMARK

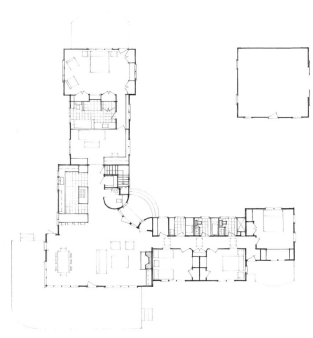

FIRST FLOOR PLAN

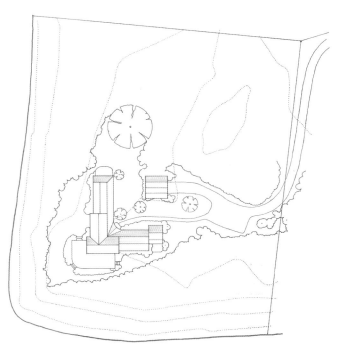

SITE PLAN

Meadow House | Zachary Hinchcliffe

with Robert Miklos FAIA / designLAB architects

EDGARTOWN

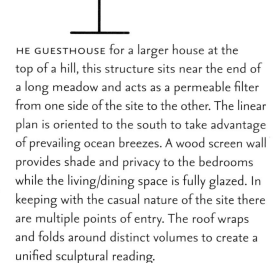HE GUESTHOUSE for a larger house at the top of a hill, this structure sits near the end of a long meadow and acts as a permeable filter from one side of the site to the other. The linear plan is oriented to the south to take advantage of prevailing ocean breezes. A wood screen wall provides shade and privacy to the bedrooms while the living/dining space is fully glazed. In keeping with the casual nature of the site there are multiple points of entry. The roof wraps and folds around distinct volumes to create a unified sculptural reading.

The materials reflect the muted palette of gray-greens found in the vegetation on the Vineyard and take into account the intense weathering that occurs on the island. The vertical wood siding is western red cedar, stained a weathered gray. The roof is standing seam lead-coated copper both for coloration and durability. The folded continuity of the roof plane finds a corollary in the floors. The bluestone floor of the north patio extends through the living area and kitchen and up to clad the chimney. On the south side of the house, a mahogany bench becomes a deck extending into the screened porch.

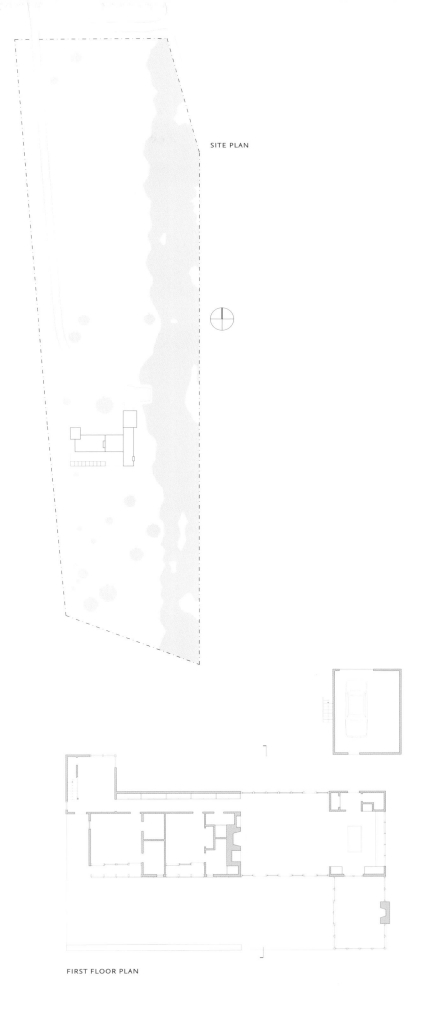

SITE PLAN

FIRST FLOOR PLAN

2006

Camp Manaquayak | Sullivan O'Connor Architects

WEST TISBURY

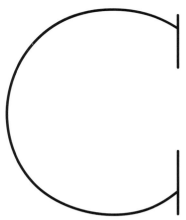

CAMP MANAQUAYAK IS LOCATED in the wooded hills of Lambert's Cove. The clients, who live in a historic house in Boston, wanted an island residence appropriate to the Vineyard style with a contemporary feel. Light, air, and privacy were important as was a connection to the site and surroundings.

The house is composed of three modules, which create a secluded courtyard. The modules are set by priority of use and site location. The "utilitarian" component defines the street edge, the "public" component is central, and the "master suite" extends toward the back of the site. The courtyard offers a quiet retreat with outdoor views on three sides.

The form is derived from local architectural precedents. Shed roofs, symbolic of a simpler past, unify the three structures. The two-story "utilitarian" wing relates to height and formal facades of the farmhouses in the area. The central wing, which encloses the main living area, forms a rectangle and serves as a link between the other two modules. A 14-foot ceiling height unifies the space and modulates the transition from two stories at the front to one story at the back. The shape of the master-suite wing is designed to convey a sense of independence and freedom.

The exterior finishes of natural color and texture work to integrate the form of the house with the wooded setting. Cedar sidewall and trim blend with the coloring and texture of tree trunks and branches along with black clad windows complementing the shadows and openings of the forest beyond. Canopy and shade are provided by a green standing seam roof.

FIRST FLOOR PLAN

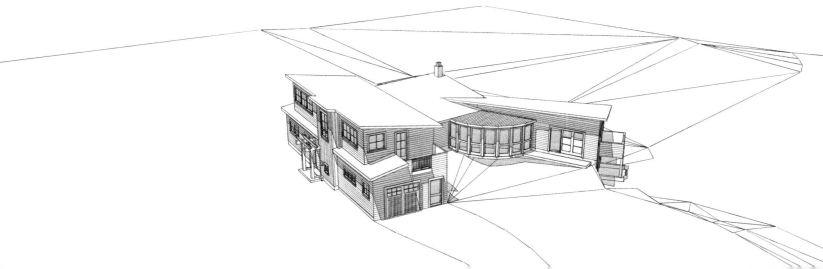

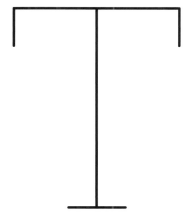

HIS HOUSE, designed for a philosophy professor, a ceramic artist, and their two children, is located on a wooded hillside in Chilmark, with distant views toward the ocean to the south and the rolling inland hills to the north. To accommodate the topography of the site, the house was broken into three volumes, each articulated as a kind of autonomous vernacular piece. These contain the living/dining space; the two-story central core of the kitchen with master bedroom above; and a bedroom wing. The volumes are connected by a flat-roofed element that expands outward near the kitchen to form the screened porch. Two freestanding structures, a small writer's cabin, and a potting studio, were also built. All of the volumes were inspired by the simple outbuildings found around the island.

The connection between inside and outside is expressed differently in each volume. The transparent living wing, set on an east-west axis to take advantage of the views, floats slightly above the sloping terrain to either side, while the barn-like bedroom wing is anchored to the uphill edge of the site, its sliding doors opening to reveal a private, porch-like hallway connecting the bedrooms to an open deck.

1991

Professor/Potter House and Studio | MacNelly Cohen Architects

CHILMARK

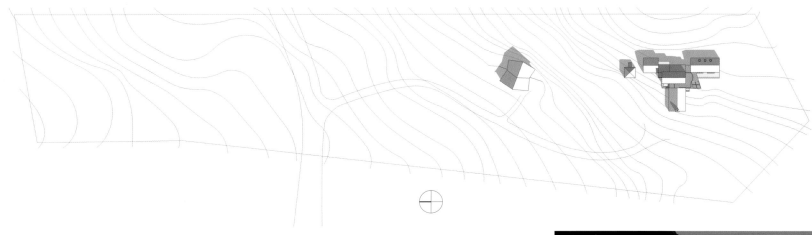

FIRST FLOOR PLAN

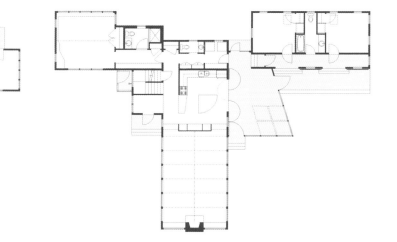

Together these wings define an outdoor space into which the angular screen porch projects. Behind this porch the kitchen wall may be opened fully in summer to create a large central space, the focal point for the life of the house. Above the kitchen, the master bedroom opens to a deck over the screened porch, with a view of the ocean to the south. A later bedroom addition, adjacent to the entry on the north side of the central volume, has views of the small front meadow through oversized double-hung windows.

Located downhill from the house, the potting studio is a play on the idea of a vessel, both as container and as object set upon an undulating surface. As container, its enclosing gesture is the roof above, seen as the inverse of the form of a bowl or pot. The studio's butterfly plan separates the work space from the kiln area, and generates the origami folds of the roof.

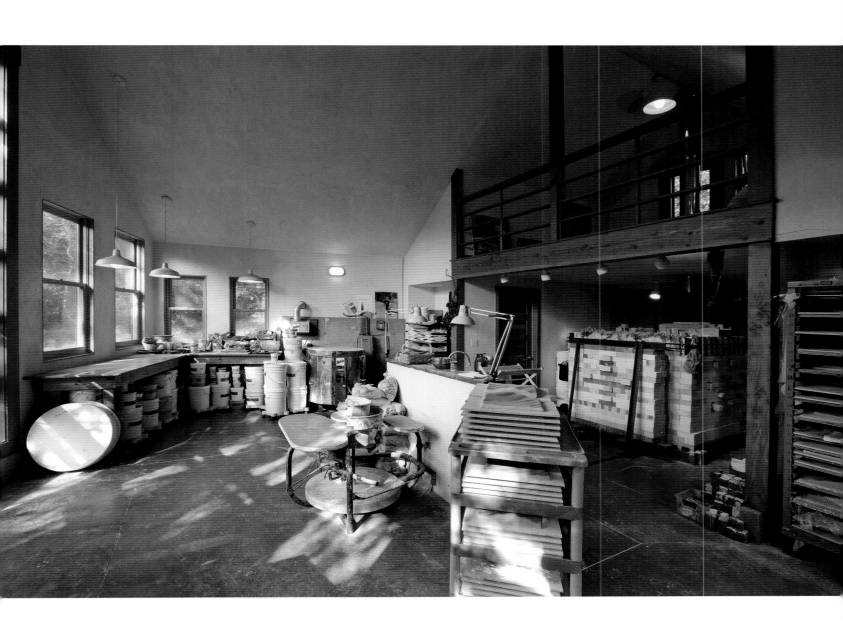

Located at the brow of a wooded hillside site, Hilltop House was designed to reconcile the goals of maximizing both energy efficiency and water views. The structure is nestled into the hillside to provide additional insulation, and the main living areas are located on the second floor to take advantage of views overlooking Lambert's Cove.

All habitable spaces have a southern exposure that is shaded in the summer by roof overhangs or balcony and deck projections. Winter sun is allowed to enter, with solar energy absorbed by polished concrete floors that act as a heat sink to store and radiate heat naturally. A trellis that will eventually be covered with wisteria will provide afternoon shade for the deck as well as the large expanse of glass in the living room. The butterfly roof of the master bedroom level collects and directs water to a garden cistern, while operable clerestory windows encourage cross ventilation and the collection of summer breezes.

Starting with stone and earth exterior terraces, the vertical circulation weaves up through the house, with stairs becoming lighter in construction as one climbs up through the trees. From the ground floor vestibule a solidly enclosed stair arrives at the main floor level facing a semi-recessed screened porch that connects the interior back to the tree-covered site. An open steel stair with black walnut treads rises to a master bedroom aerie, which overlooks the living room and the water views beyond. A private balcony off the bedroom provides an intimate refuge in the treetops.

Warm brown concrete exterior walls and wood cedar siding blend with the natural colors of the woods. Chosen for economy, ease of maintenance, and thermal mass, the cast-in-place concrete walls and floors create an earthy fossil-like texture using local sand and aggregates.

2009

Hilltop House | Weiss + Reed Architects

WEST TISBURY

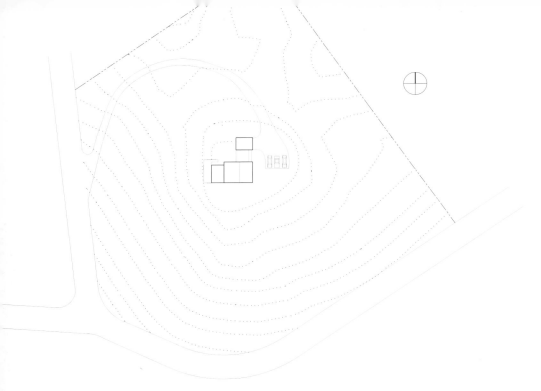

SITE PLAN

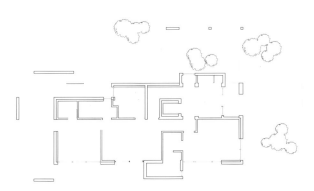

FIRST FLOOR PLAN

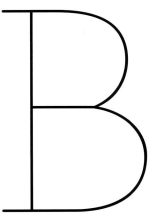

BUILT IN THE FOOTPRINT of a former boat repair shop, Quitsa House is located on a tidal saltwater pond. The modest property includes a dock and a ramp for swimming and launching kayaks and rowboats.

From the street, Quitsa House appears to be an unpretentious shingled cottage with no hint of the openness within. The property is surrounded on three sides by a weathered board fence that creates the feeling of a very private courtyard. The exterior space between the cottage and the dock is furnished like an outdoor room. Adirondack chairs provide seating on the covered porch. A table on the covered porch and a picnic table closer to the dock provide for informal outdoor dining. A boardwalk links the dock to the lawn that borders the cottage.

The first floor of Quitsa House contains a main room for dining and living, served by a galley kitchen. Daylight fills the space through wall-to-wall sliding doors that face the pond. The entire wall of the dining end is an installation by sculptor Andy Goldsworthy. The opposite wall in the living area is dominated by a fireplace constructed of pieces of stacked slate.

On the second floor are three bedrooms, two of which open onto a second-floor balcony with a view of the pond. The stairway between the first and second floors is lined with a built-in bookcase on the exterior wall.

The materials throughout the cottage are joined together in a minimalist fashion. The living/dining room walls are natural western hemlock, the ceiling beams are natural fir, and the floor is limestone.

SITE PLAN

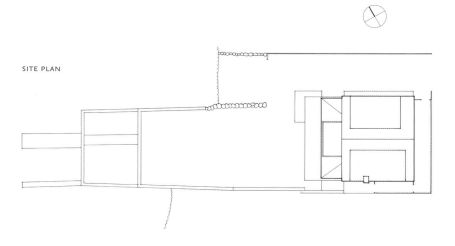

FIRST FLOOR PLAN

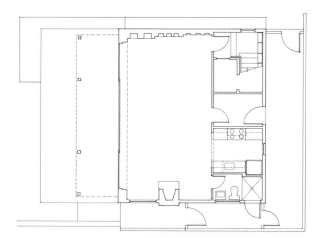

Meadow House | Patrick R. Crosgrove, Architect

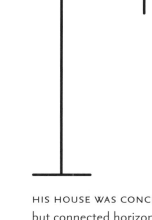

T HIS HOUSE WAS CONCEIVED as three distinct but connected horizontal pavilions intended to rest on the site with minimal impact. The main pavilion at the center has an open floor plan that accommodates kitchen, dining, and living areas. Large sliding glass doors open onto decks bringing the outdoors inside to create a bright, airy interior with sweeping distant views. The secondary pavilions, containing bedrooms and baths, are located at opposite ends of the living area to provide privacy and to enclose exterior spaces. Decks on each side of the structure allow guests to experience the natural settings and vistas, while maintaining an unusual sense of personal space in a house of this scale. All areas have multiple glass sliding doors that are used as large windows for maximum light and full ventilation. Cooled by the distant ocean breeze, the house is sited to take full advantage of the changing landscape.

Zoning limits on size and height were ultimately an advantage to the final design, supporting its minimal intrusion on the site. The suggestion of an almost flat roof strengthens the horizontal design and benefits the neighbors by keeping the profile low and unassuming.

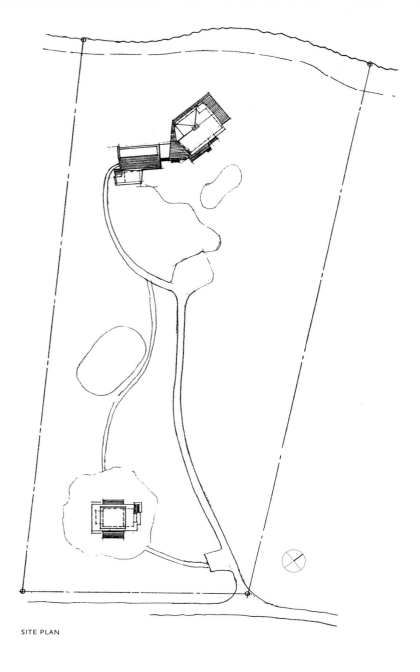

SITE PLAN

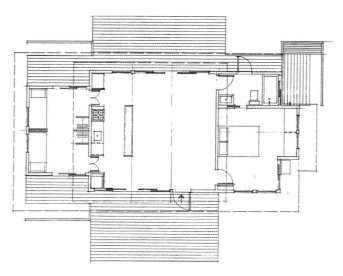

FIRST FLOOR PLAN

2008

The Sugar Mill | Hutker Architects

CHILMARK

S

UGAR MILL SITS at the top of Squibnocket Hill with views of the Atlantic and Menemsha Pond.

A series of hipped roof volumes reflects the different aspects of the program, each incorporating different levels of natural light and specific views.

Marking the entrance is a stone ellipse (The Sugar Mill), which is designed to be seen as a continuous inside/outside element interrupting an otherwise transparent corner of glass.

On the interior subtle combinations of contemporary materials and detailing are juxtaposed with more traditional elements, while the use of teak, cedar, and copper on the exterior has given the house an immediate weathered and timeless appearance.

The landscape has been re-interpreted through the cultivation and restoration of its indigenous plant materials, interrupted only by a view deck off of the living room and an integrated lap pool to the east.

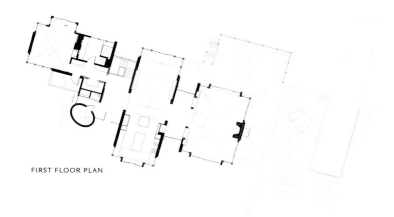
FIRST FLOOR PLAN

GUESTHOUSE PLAN

Tashmoo Residence | Breese Architects

S

URROUNDED BY FIELDS and farms, this house is set in a secluded cove adjacent to Lake Tashmoo. The landscape is gradually revealed on the approach to the house down a mossy stone path. From the front door there is a focused view of the cove. Beyond the entry foyer is a dramatic living room, flooded with natural light and focused on a wall of water-side windows.

The master suite stretches the full length of the second floor, taking advantage of the southern exposure and framing a layered view of Vineyard Sound to the north. Two detached bedroom suites are connected to the main house by a covered walkway and a screened porch.

A palette of raw and durable materials exposes a structure that will wear to a fine patina. Splitface granite columns support a cedar truss clad in zinc-coated metal. The gabled forms and woven shingle exterior are punctuated by deeply set copper clad windows and doors. The interiors echo this approach to material with tinted concrete floors, exposed steel, and unpainted plaster surfaces. The staircase is detailed with thin steel components, complemented by wood treads and handrails.

SITE PLAN

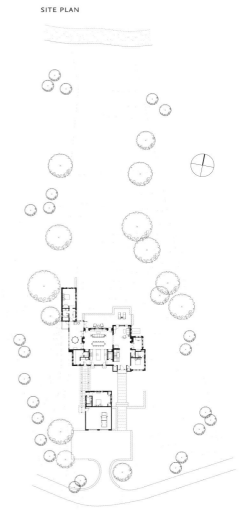

FIRST FLOOR PLAN

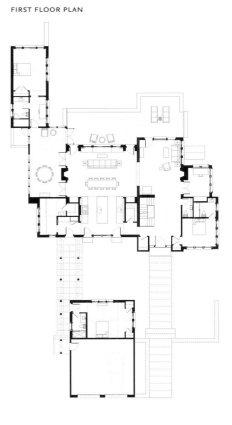

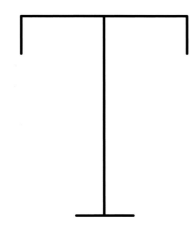

THE RURAL SITE on the brow of the hill offers panoramic views of both the Atlantic and Squibnocket Pond. Capturing these two views was paramount to the success of this house.

The site was large but very restricted, with a maximum height of eighteen feet, measured from historic grade and a tight building envelope. This meant that the house would spread out with "tentacles" toward the spectacular views. The idea that there had once been barns on the land and that there could be remnants of old foundations on which to build the house proved unfounded, but still offered an interesting concept for the design. The new house would stretch along the brow of the hill, and as seen from below look like a series of agrarian buildings that had always been there. Modest from a distance, the buildings would become more complex as the detailing emerged.

The plan is as open as possible, with visual axis playing an important part in the overall scheme. The detailing has a Shaker feel to it. Clean and open on the inside, the house retains a more traditional vernacular on the outside.

2000

Chilmark House | Shope Reno Wharton

CHILMARK

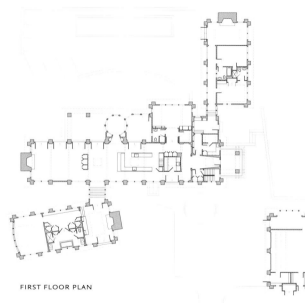

FIRST FLOOR PLAN

SITE PLAN

Aquinnah House | Hecht and Associates Architects

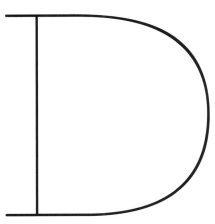

ESIGNED FOR THE ARCHITECT'S MOTHER, Aquinnah House overlooks Vineyard Sound from its perch atop secondary dunes surrounded by scrub oak, wild roses, and beach plum. The new home complements a 1940s fisherman's cottage next door where the client's children and grandchildren spend their summers.

This was one of the first houses to be constructed in the town of Aquinnah after a one-year building moratorium and enactment of new zoning regulations aimed at reducing the impact of new construction on the fragile dune and wetland habitats characteristic of the area. The new building code included strict height limitations and aesthetic guidance to minimize the visibility of new construction.

With this house, the siting was carefully worked out to minimize impact on the environment; every effort was made to preserve existing trees, woody shrubs, and beach grasses. The arrangement of spaces forms a long (115 feet), single-story, narrow structure sited along the back edge of the dunes and consisting of three main forms joined by smaller shed-roof connectors. These links serve as entry points and permit the gabled sleeping and living rooms

to follow the topography and fit among the oaks that shelter the house from view. By breaking the house into smaller elements with full height ceilings, the design capitalizes on the strict height limitations imposed by zoning regulations. A north-facing deck increases the footprint by about 50 percent and provides outdoor entertaining space; part of the deck steps up in elevation to attain a full view of the ocean.

In keeping with older houses in the area, the exterior forms are simple shapes clad in traditional wood shingles. The interior is centered on a large open living/dining/kitchen space framed with site-built trusses made of light wood framing bolted with concealed steel plates. Otherwise, the finishes are understated. Awning and double-hung windows on both south- and north-facing elevations, in combination with ceiling fans, provide ample air circulation to cool the space. Bamboo flooring is used throughout the central living area and bedrooms while blue-green floor tiles at the entry and kitchen reinforce the relationship to the sea. The house has an ease and informality, a place where grandchildren are always welcome to play.

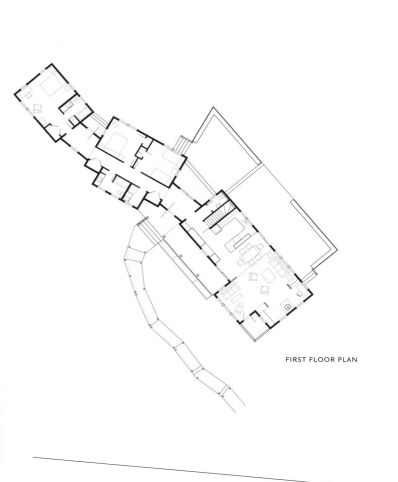

FIRST FLOOR PLAN

SITE PLAN

Groove House | Charles Rose Architects

T

HE SITE FOR THIS MODEST HOUSE is on the north slope of a wooded property with views of Vineyard Sound. This project makes every effort to embed the occupant in the natural environment. The topography is steep, sloping a full story between a grassy clearing to the south of the building and woods to the north. The house, small and compact, defines the southern edge of an intimate open space—similar to a small boat tracing a path within a powerful seascape. The circulation plan, porch, and roof deck heighten the experience of the outdoors, encouraging interaction and exploration through routes and outlooks that provide sweeping views to the east, west, and north and glimpses of the distant Sound.

There are two bedrooms at opposite ends of the house, each with its own bathroom. A small communal area—with a kitchenette, eating area, and a sitting room that doubles as a third bedroom—is located at the center, adjacent to the entry. A curtain can be drawn between the kitchen area and the sitting area for greater privacy. The design incorporates abundant natural light throughout, filtered in part by the surrounding trees, creating airy spaces in counterpoint to the rich teak, mahogany, and cork interior palette. The exterior material palette includes pigmented concrete, stone, copper, cedar, and fir, linking it to the main house (p. 168) and the New England region.

FIRST FLOOR PLAN

SITE PLAN

LONG HOUSE IS SITED on the gently sloping shores of Tiah's Cove, just outside the one-hundred-foot buffer zone from the inland edge of the Tisbury Great Pond wetlands. The house is composed of two wings shifted to break up the mass, one with the kitchen/family room and screen porch, the other with the living room and library. Each wing is a traditional gabled structure with shed dormers to accommodate the bedrooms above. The aged natural cedar trim and shingles has allowed the mass of the house to blend into the landscape over time.

One of the main objectives of the design was for the first floor to maintain an openness both within the house and to the outdoors. From the entry there is a view to the pond beyond. Oversized doors allow the kitchen/family room to spill out to a long open porch along the pond and to a generous screened porch on the swimming pool side. Inside, a 10-foot ceiling height is maintained throughout the first floor, but the house conforms to the overall 24-foot height restriction in the area.

Long House | Michael Barclay

FIRST FLOOR PLAN

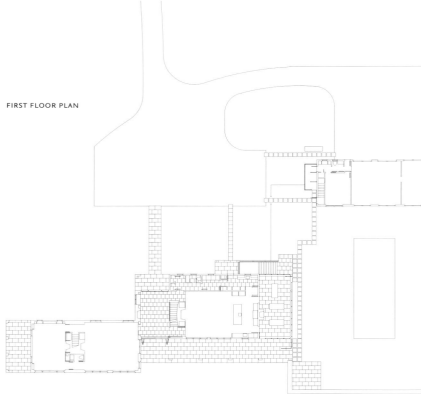

HIS GARDEN POOL HOUSE and pavilion complement Vineyard outdoor living. Located on a thirty-five-acre family equestrian farm, the pool house, pavilion, and landscape are part of a larger site master plan. The new building and structures establish a strong aesthetic and stylistic direction for future renovations on the site while offering the family a complete living environment for their seasonal visits. Linear forms, clean lines, and a restrained palette of materials are represented in the landscape and building.

The structures are anchored to a low bluestone wall at the base of a series of lawn terraces. Teak windows allow natural light to filter into the pickled fir changing rooms, limestone bathroom, and teak, soapstone, and copper prep kitchen. In contrast to the solid, grounded pool house, the adjoining pavilion is open on all sides providing living, dining, and kitchen spaces for the pool terrace.

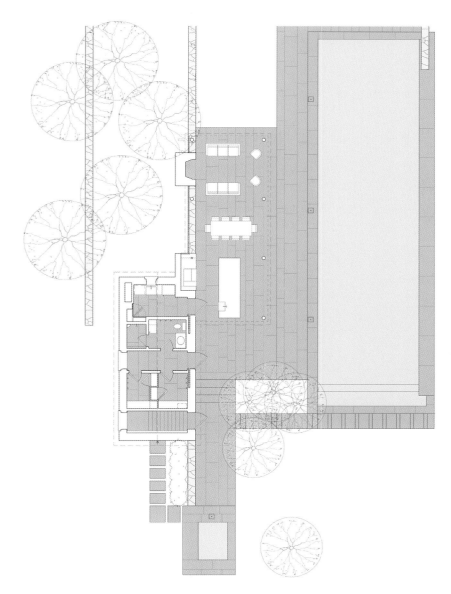

FIRST FLOOR PLAN

Little Camp | Albert, Righter & Tittmann Architects

CHAPPAQUIDDICK

ıTTLE CAMP IS ADJACENT to an old, slightly ramshackle "camp" with exposed rafter tails, open studs, and tree-trunk porch posts. After renting—and loving—that camp for years, the family had a chance to build a home for themselves next door. In Little Camp they wanted to capture the spirit of the old camp. The new house also has exposed rafter tails, an interior of wood, and tree trunk porch posts.

Little Camp responds to the shared feeling on Chappaquiddick for informality, a low building profile, and muted colors. The house is vernacular in character, strongly horizontal in emphasis with a low eave line, and sheathed in gray shingles with gray-green trim.

The rafter tails are cut in the shape of stylized fish heads in recognition of a favorite island sport. Little Camp, unlike the old camp next door, can be occupied year round, but it is geared to informal summer living, with provisions

for fishing and boating equipment, an outdoor shower, and an expansive living porch with many points of access from the house.

The plan of Little Camp is largely one room deep to encourage cross ventilation and to take advantage of water views to the north while also admitting sunlight from the south. To keep the building profile low, the second floor bedrooms are contained within the roof, which is a gambrel on the entry side but sweeps down in an uninterrupted single pitch on the water side.

The long, low main house is complemented by a compact guesthouse and a separate garage/workshop with compatible but simplified details.

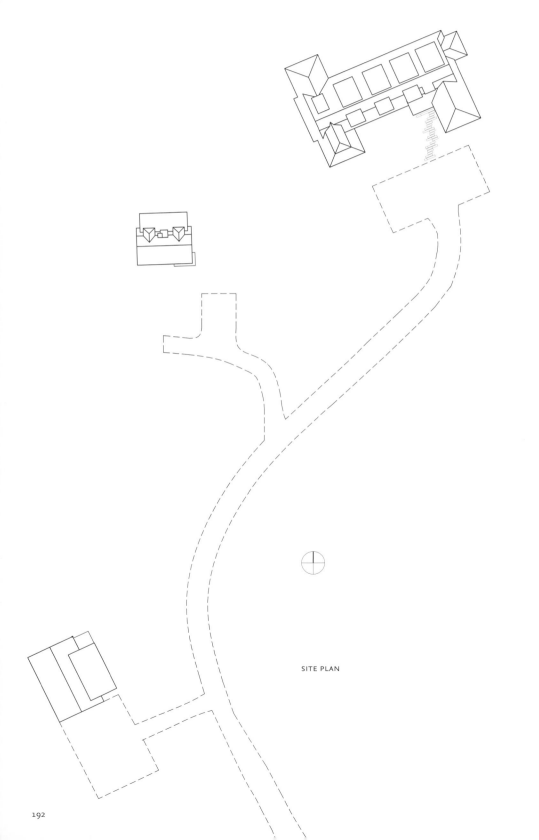

SITE PLAN

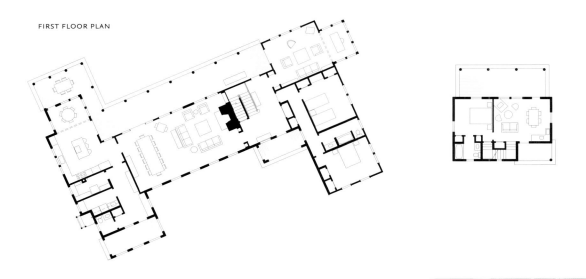

THIS HOUSE IS LOCATED at the end of a long dirt road that ascends a hill with distant views to the north over Vineyard Sound to the Elizabeth Islands. The house becomes visible halfway up the hill. Its most prominent feature from that perspective is the long aluminum pergola, which soon will be covered with trumpet vines. When lit at night, the continuous row of second-floor windows acts like a lantern.

To accommodate a couple with two grown children, two grandchildren, and more to come, there are four bedrooms on the second floor. On the first floor is a master bedroom suite, a study, and a large room that contains a living area, kitchen, and dining room. The kitchen in this space is like a large walk-in closet, with more than adequate work space and storage. A suspended track system provides most of the lighting and unifies the space. Side alcoves containing a long window seat, a breakfast area, and a buffet, break down the scale. The room is serene in its finishes (white bead board ceilings, hickory floors, bleached cedar walls, and maple cabinets) but assertive in proportions and dimensions—55 feet long, almost 18 feet wide, and 10 feet high.

To reduce its overall scale, the house was designed to appear as if it might have been built in two phases. At its core is a two-story, rectangular volume, with a large, bracketed, overhanging eave. It is clad in a rusticated pattern of repeating watertables. On three sides that volume is wrapped with predominantly one-story elements clad in cedar shingles. The pergola extends the full length of the north elevation.

SITE PLAN

FIRST FLOOR PLAN

Cliff House | Steven Blatt Architects

CHILMARK

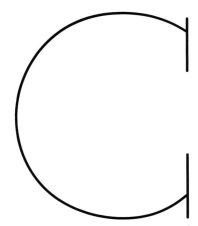

LIFF HOUSE SITS NEAR the edge of the Wequobsque Cliffs, close to the highest point on the Vineyard. Like the twisted, wind-swept oak trees on the site, the house spreads outward, hunkered down against the elements. The owners' desire for an informal, compound-like ambience coupled with building height restrictions dictated the meandering, horizontal quality of the plan.

The building archetypes found up-island are simple and straightforward, functional and appropriate, of the land and of the sea. The design borrows from these vernacular forms and combines them in response to the particular features of the site and requirements of the program.

The house is composed of three distinct structures: a timber-framed "barn" or living area; an exposed-wood-trussed main house for cooking and dining, with a smaller, informal gathering area; and a building for sleeping and bathing. The three buildings are connected by short, light-filled interior hallways and an

expansive exterior deck. In plan, the compound forms a gentle arc, embracing visitors arriving on the landward side and opening to panoramic ocean vistas on the deck side. Traditional exterior forms and details juxtapose a modernist approach to interior spatial relationships.

All materials were selected to stand the test of time in a harsh marine environment. White and red cedar shingles and red cedar trim were left to weather naturally. Exterior paint, used as a colorful accent, is limited to window sash and doors. An equally high level of finish and durability is realized on the interior, including Douglas fir walls and ceilings, antique Heart Pine flooring, soapstone counters, numerous custom built-ins, and a timber-framed "barn" with stress-skin panels beneath the vernacular wood sheathing.

Now that the house has weathered to a silvery gray and native plantings have filled in, the owner's hope that the house would "seem timeless, as if having been fixed upon its country landscape a long time ago" has been fulfilled.

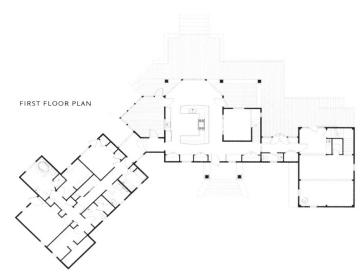

FIRST FLOOR PLAN

Martha's Vineyard House | Architecture Research Office

M

ARTHA'S VINEYARD HOUSE is situated against a gentle hill at the southern edge of a clearing in the woods, which offers an expansive view of the water. Three blocks containing different domestic programs are arranged to define a series of exterior spaces, including a protected entry court partially enclosed by the adjacent wooded slope. Two perpendicular, L-shaped walls clad in cedar siding define the north and south blocks. Their horizontality, depth, and texture accentuate the connection of the house to the site. The detailing of these walls, using two different widths and depths of specially-milled wood boards, achieves shadows similar to those cast by the surrounding scrub oak trees. A laser cutter was a critical tool employed to explore phenomena of light, shadow, pattern, and texture in the design of these walls. Contrasting in scale and orientation are the standing seam zinc siding and the wood windows.

SITE PLAN

FIRST FLOOR PLAN

Credits

Aquinnah House
Hecht and Associates, Architects
Contractor: Pizzano Construction
Photographer: Warren Jagger Photography

Bluff House
Maryann Thompson Architects
Contractor: Weiss Construction
Photographers: Chuck Choi, Jessica Springer,
Steve Turner

Camp Manaquayak
Sullivan O'Connor Architects
Contractor: Laurence Clancy Construction
Photographer: Meg Bodnar

Chilmark House
Shope Reno Wharton
Contractor: John G. Early Contractor and
Builder
Photographer: Durston Saylor

Cliff House
Steven Blatt
Contractor: John G. Early Contractor and
Builder
Photographer: Brian Vanden Brink

Garden Pool House and Pavilion
Jill Neubauer Architects
Contractor: Doyle Construction
Photographer: Charles Mayer

Groove House
Charles Rose Architects
Contractor: Andrew A. Flake, Inc.
Photographer: Bruce Martin

Highland House
Rick Sundberg/Olson Kundig Architects
Contractor: Andrew A. Flake, Inc.
Photographers: Roger Foley, Peter Vander-
warter, Charles Mayer, Eric Piasecki

Hilltop House
Weiss + Reed Architects
Contractor: David Knauf Construction, Inc.
Photographer: Greg Premru

Little Camp
Albert, Righter & Tittmann Architects
Contractor: Doyle Construction
Photographer: Brian Vanden Brink

Long House
Michael Barclay
Contractor: Mark Hurwitz
Photographer: Sydney Bachman

Martha's Vineyard House
Architecture Research Office
Photographers: Elizabeth Felicella and
Thomas Brodin

Meadow House
Patrick R. Cosgrove, Architect
Contractor: Building Shelter
Photographer: Gil Jacobs

Meadow House
Zachary Hinchliffe with Robert Miklos FAIA/
designLAB architects
Contractor: CEDCo
Photographer: Peter Vanderwarker

MVII
Moskow Linn Architects
Contractor: McGrath Carpentry Service
Photographer: Greg Premu

Point House
Hart Associates Architects
Contractor: Serpa Brothers Construction
Photographer: Cheryle St. Onge

Pond House
South Mountain Company
Photographer: Brian Vanden Brink

Professor/Potter House and Studio
MacNelly Cohen Architects
Contractor, house: John Alexander
Contractor, studio: William Meegan Fine
Carpentry
Photographer: Peter Vanderwarker

Quitsa House
Krueger Associates
Contractor: William Meegan Fine Carpentry
Photographer: Brian Vanden Brink

Snow Point
Hutker Architects
Contractor: Bob Avakian
Photographer: Brian Vanden Brink

Stonewall Beach Residence
Office of Peter Rose
Contractor: Andrew A. Flake, Inc.
Photographer: Peter Vanderwarker

The Sugar Mill
Hutker Architects
Contractor: Johnson Builders, LLC
Photographer: Brian Vanden Brink

Tashmoo Residence
Breese Architects
Contractor: Baumhofer Builders
Photographer: Shannon Reddy

Trellis House
Handlin Garrahan Zachos and Associates
Contractor: Cornerstone Builders
Photographer: Peter Vanderwarker

VHR10 gHouse
Darren Petrucci, AIA
Photographer: Bill Timmerman

Acknowledgments

Thanks to the architects who designed the houses, contributed the photographs and wrote essays describing their projects for *Martha's Vineyard: Contemporary Living*. Without the architects' expertise, the fine work of the builders, and the vision of the clients, this publication would not be possible.

Thanks to our associate Sarah West who provided thoughtful insight on the book's development and was responsible for much of its organization.

Thanks to the professionals at The Monacelli Press, especially our editor Elizabeth White, who shepherded the book from initial concept through distribution, and to book designer David Blankenship.

And a special thanks to our families, including Allison, Erin, Zac, Jake, Jackson, and Ava, who is supportive in every way and enjoy spending time on Martha's Vineyard as much as we do.

Published in the United States by The Monacelli Press,
a division of Random House, Inc., New York

The Monacelli Press and the M design are registered
trademarks of Random House, Inc.

Library of Congress PCN Control number: 2010920703

10 9 8 7 6 5 4 3 2 1
First edition

Printed in China

Designed by David Blankenship

Typeset in Seria Sans

www.monacellipress.com

Photography Credits
Sydney Bachman: 172–181
Meg Bodnar: 92–97
Chuck Choi: 4–5, 48–51, 168
Elizabeth Felicella and Thomsa Brodin: Cover, 213–219
Roger Foley: 20
Gil Jacobs: 128–133
Warren Jagger Photography: 161–165
Brian Martin: 167, 169–171
Charles Mayer: 24–25, 182–189
Greg Premu: 6, 32, 35–43, 108–117
Shannon Reddy: 142–149
Cheryle St. Onge: 52–61
Durston Saylor: 150–159
Bill Timmerman: Back cover, 70–79
Trends Publishing International/Eric Piasecki: 29, 31 bottom
Steve Turner: 44, 47
Brian Vanden Brink: 63–69, 80–85, 118–127, 134–141, 191,
192–197
Peter Vanderwarker: 2–3, 10–19, 23, 26, 28, 30, 31 top, 87–91,
98–107, 198–205, 206, 208–211